CAT Files

Snow Leopard

WRITTEN BY
BETHANY LATHAM

KidHaven PUBLISHING

Published in 2027 by
KidHaven Publishing, an Imprint of Greenhaven Publishing, LLC
2544 Clinton St., Buffalo, NY 14224

Written by: Bethany Latham
Edited by: Rebecca Phillips-Bartlett
Designed by: Ker Ker Lee

Cataloging-in-Publication Data
Names: Latham, Bethany.
Title: Snow leopard / Bethany Latham.
Description: Buffalo, NY : KidHaven Publishing, 2027. | Series: Cat files | Includes glossary and index.
Identifiers: ISBN 9781534569621 (pbk.) | ISBN 9781534569638 (library bound) | ISBN 9781534569645 (ebook)
Subjects: LCSH: Snow leopard--Juvenile literature. | Snow leopard--Behavior--Juvenile literature. | Snow leopard--Habitat--Juvenile literature.
Classification: LCC QL737.C23 L384 2027 | DDC 599.7555--dc23

Printed in China

CPSIA compliance information: Batch #QS27KH: For further information contact Greenhaven Publishing LLC at 1-844-317-7404.

Please visit our website, www.greenhavenpublishing.com. For a free color catalog of all our high-quality books, call toll free 1-844-317-7404 or fax 1-844-317-7405.

Find us on

Photo Credits – Images courtesy of Shutterstock.com, unless otherwise stated.

Cover & Recurring – Eric Isselee, Maksim Nafikov, AminaStock, BMR Creation, graficriver_icons_logo, Vector Tradition. 2–3 – David Havel. 4–5 – Warren Metcalf, Stu Porter, Howard Darby, Michal Ninger. 6–7 – Adrian Dockerty, Stefan Rankovic. 8–9 – Nimedly, Ravneesh Singh Klair. 10–11 – Eric Isseleel. 12–13 – KMW Photography, POUSSINFRANCAIS, Ondrej Prosicky. 14–15 – Shivang Mehta, ABIR ROY BARMAN, Wirestock Creators, Holly S Cannon. 16–17 – Ondrej Prosicky, Holly S Cannons. 18–19 – Kwadrat, Uzo Borewicz. 20–21 – Holly S Cannon. 22–23 – Holly S Cannon.

Contents

Words that look like this can be found in the glossary on page 24.

Big Cats

Big cats are powerful predators. Predators hunt the animals they eat. Animals that eat other animals are called carnivores. Scientists group big cats together because they have lots in common, such as sharp claws.

Lion

Snow leopard

All cats are in the Felidae animal family. This family includes smaller groups. The Pantherinae group includes big cats, such as snow leopards, tigers, and lions. The Felinae group includes cheetahs and smaller cats.

Tiger

Cheetah

FACT FILE

DIET:	Carnivore
ANIMAL TYPE:	Mammal
HUNTING:	Predator

Snow Leopards

Snow leopards live in 12 different Asian countries, including China and India. Snow leopards are very shy and hard to find. They are known as the "ghosts of the mountains."

Unlike other big cats, snow leopards cannot roar.

FACT FILE

CONTINENT:	Asia
SIZE:	Around 35 to 51 inches (90 to 130 cm) long (without tail)
WEIGHT:	Usually between 50 and 90 pounds (23 and 41 kg)
SPEED:	Up to 40 miles (65 km) per hour

Habitat

An animal's habitat is its natural home. Snow leopards live high up in the mountains across Asia. These include the Himalayas. They often live up to 16,000 feet (5,000 m) above the sea.

Snow leopards usually live in places where trees cannot grow. Instead of trees, snow leopards use rocky shelves and cliffs to hide themselves while hunting. A snow leopard's habitat is very cold and dry.

Snow leopards' nostrils warm up the air they breathe.

Body

Snow leopards all have these important body parts:

Snow leopard fur is thick and long for warmth.

Snow leopards' back legs are longer than their front legs. Their strong legs help them leap very far.

Snow leopards' tails can be 3.3 feet (1 m) long.

Snow leopards have wide noses and nostrils.

Snow leopards have gray or green eyes.

Snow leopards have large, wide paws. This helps them walk on snow.

Blending In

A snow leopard's fur helps it camouflage itself. Its fur is yellowish grey in summer. This helps the snow leopard blend in with the rocks. In winter, its fur becomes almost white to match the snow.

There is a snow leopard in this picture!

FACT FILE

COLOR:	Pale gray
PATTERN:	Spotted rose shapes
FUR LENGTH:	Long
CAMOUFLAGE TYPE:	Concealing and seasonal

Snow leopards have spotted, rose-shaped markings. These markings look like shadows on the rocks, which makes snow leopards harder to see. This is called concealing camouflage.

Hunting Prey

Snow leopards eat animals such as blue sheep, ibex, and deer. Snow leopards can kill prey up to three times heavier than themselves. Snow leopards' long tails help them balance when hunting.

Ibex

Blue sheep

Snow leopards usually hunt once every eight to ten days.

Snow leopards are ambush hunters. This means they quietly sneak up on their prey, then attack. Snow leopards usually ambush their prey from above.

FACT FILE

TAIL LENGTH: Around 3.3 feet (1 m)

TEETH LENGTH: Up to 1.2 inches (3 cm)

PREY SIZE: Up to three times body weight

Family Life

Snow leopards usually live alone. Groups of animals often have their own names. Groups of snow leopards are so rare that they have no group name. Adult snow leopards usually only get together to mate.

Snow leopards move around a lot to find food. They can travel up to 25 miles (40 km) in one night. Snow leopards communicate using urine and claw marks. This is called scent marking.

FACT FILE

GROUP NAME:	None
GROUP SIZE:	Usually solitary
COMMUNICATION:	Scent marking

Raising Young

Baby snow leopards are called cubs. The mother is usually pregnant for around three months. She usually has two or three cubs. The mother makes a shelter for her cubs using her own fur.

FACT FILE

NAME:	Cub
NUMBER:	Usually two to three
PREGNANCY LENGTH:	Around three months
WHEN FULLY GROWN:	Two to four years

Cubs usually stay with their mother for one to two years. Cubs become adults at two to four years old.

Cats in Danger

Scientists label snow leopards as vulnerable. This means the number of snow leopards is falling. The main danger to snow leopards is human activity. Some humans hunt snow leopards for their fur and bones.

Some humans also hunt snow leopards' prey. This means there are fewer animals for the snow leopards to eat. Many people around the world are trying to protect the snow leopards.

Cat Files

Snow leopards are beautiful big cats. They are well-suited to their cold habitat. Do you think you would like to see a snow leopard in the wild?

Roar-Some Roundup

CONTINENT:	Asia
HABITAT:	Mountains
FUR LENGTH:	Long
CAMOUFLAGE TYPE:	Concealing and seasonal
HUNTING STYLE:	Ambush

Big cats play a very important role in nature. They need to be protected. Maybe you can do some research with a grown-up about how to help snow leopards!

Glossary

camouflage to hide by blending into the surroundings

communicate to pass information between two or more things

mammal an animal that is warm-blooded, has a backbone, and makes milk to feed their young

mate to make babies with an animal of the same species

nostrils two holes in the nose that an animal breathes through

pregnant when a female animal has one or more babies growing inside her

prey animals that are hunted by other animals for food

seasonal changing or happening during different seasons or times of year

Index